Progress TWIN-CAR

For most of the 1970s, the 1980s and into the 1990s, the Twin Car trams were very much the forgotten part of the Blackpool fleet. While the Brush Cars and Balloon Cars made up the bulk of the main operational fleet, with their colourful liveries, ongoing repaints and refurbishments, the Twin Cars were always in the shadows, rarely used and often neglected. Although operation patterns varied year on year, the ongoing decline in tram passengers more or less relegated Twin Car operation to the peak summer and even then it was usually only on Market Tuesdays to Fleetwood and Illumination Saturdays. Repaints into the modern green and cream livery in the 1990s, complete with pantographs for the motor cars, did little to change this regime. Then, out of the blue, following the ban on double deckers to Fleetwood, the 2002-2004 period saw the rebirth of these trams. Allocated to the timetabled service and with five sets painted in the colourful but fictitious Metro livery, the Twin Cars ruled supreme. By 2009 it was all over, with the Fleetwood Tuesday passengers lost to the Line 1 bus, just three sets were used during the year, on only a handful of occasions. For 2010, just two sets have been made available for service and with the Supertrams now on the horizon, 2011 is expected to be the final year of operation for the Twin Car. For a class of tram car that is supposed to be unpopular with crews, difficult to operate and often frowned upon, 2010 marks 50 years of service.

Welcome to the first book in a new series which will look at each class of Blackpool tram in detail. Having gained a cult following in recent years, the Progress Twin Car seems an appropriate place to begin. The Editor would like to thank all the people who submitted photographs, including Vic Nutton, Tony Wilson of Travel Lens Photographic, James Millington, David Umpleby, Jason Cross and Philip Higgs. A special thank you goes to Paul Turner and his father Brian, for inspiration and great assistance with the story of the early development of the Twin Cars.

Enjoy the book.
Nick Meskell, Series Editor
May 2010

*Cover: The Twin Cars were real people movers and this 1989 shot of 671+681 and 673+683 at Fleetwood Ferry on market day specials shows how these 114 seat sets could soon clear the queues. **Opposite:** From obscurity to notoriety and the Metro colours, 675+685 storm south from Little Bispham on an enthusiasts special on 2nd May 2009. 672+682 can be seen behind. (Nick Meskell x 2)*

INTRODUCTION

Although a common continental practice, trailer operation has never really caught on in the UK. Blackpool is one of the very few operators to have tried it, though it took many years for regular operation to come to fruition.

The first attempt dates as far back as the tramway itself. When opened in 1885 the line ran on the conduit system. Eight double deck cars were used, built in four pairs by two manufacturers, each pair being different. 3 and 4 were short cars primarily for winter use and during the summer were to tow single deck trailers (9 and 10) to provide the necessary capacity. Unfortunately the tramway company (it was not bought by the council until 1892) bought the trailers before it obtained permission to run them. Relations with the council were strained and they were swayed by heavy representations from local cab drivers and ruled against trailer operation on safety grounds. 9 and 10 saw some use as horse drawn cars on the conduit line but by 1891 they had been replaced by a further two motor cars.

When the North Station to Fleetwood route was constructed by the Blackpool and Fleetwood Tramroad Company in 1898 it was much in the mould of the Manx Electric Railway (as it is now known) on the Isle of Man - a successful trailer operator. In addition to ten crossbench cars the Tramroad Company purchased three similar trailers to provide extra capacity at busy times. Although they are known to have operated in 1898/99 they were soon withdrawn due to difficulties with their operation and restrictions placed on them by the Board of Trade. By 1907 they had been rebuilt as motorised cars.

Trailer operation came back on the agenda once Blackpool Corporation had taken over the Tramroad in 1920. It was proposed to introduce trailers and to provide loops at both termini of the former Tramroad route. One at Fleetwood emerged in 1925, while at North Station trams would divert down Queen Street and return to Gynn Square via the Promenade. The latter was never constructed, although trams did run down Talbot Road and out along the Promenade during track relaying in 1923. By this time the proposed trailer operation had been quietly forgotten about. There was an experiment with multiple unit control using ex-Tramroad cars 121+122 in 1924 but these did not run in passenger service.

The Twin Car has served Blackpool for over 50 years. Although the concept was soon changed to permanently couple the cars, this is a credible achievement and the longest sustained period of trailer car operation in the UK. This 1999 shot shows 672+682 fresh from the Paint Shop after accident repairs to the trailer. (Brian Turner)

THE 1957 EXPERIMENT

If Walter Luff was the manager renowned for the Streamliners then Joe Franklin must take credit for the Twin Cars. He led the party which visited Zurich in October 1957 to examine trailer operation, which is so common in Switzerland. Franklin was accompanied by Stanley Holmes (his rolling stock engineer) and two councillors on the four day trip as guests of the Chief Engineer of Zurich's Tramway. Zurich made extensive use of trailers to cope with sudden peaks in operation - indeed its last were only retired in 2007. Back in the 1950s, at busy times motor cars would pause outside one of the many depots where a small shunting loco would push one or two trailers onto the main line for connection to the rear of the motor. The process took around two minutes to complete and the tram could then resume its journey ready for the forthcoming influx of passengers.

Franklin was impressed with the high standard of turnout and presentation and was perhaps envious of the level of revenue achieved to fund overhauls and renovations of the 267 motor cars and 276 trailers. With the public willing to stand, a single tram and trailer could carry 200 passengers with three staff, compared to 90 on a Blackpool Balloon (84 seats and 6 standing). One wonders what might have occurred had Franklin seen the articulated cars then being introduced in Amsterdam.

Some time before this visit, two Railcoaches had been selected for conversion to a prototype Twin set. 275 and 276 were taken into the works in February 1957. They received a full overhaul but the most significant change was the removal of the pointed ends and their replacement with Coronation-style flat ends and Auster windscreens with Sundym visors. Unlike the production cars described later the ends were panelled wholly in metal - the later cars having fibreglass corners and domes. 275 was to be the trailer and was stripped of equipment but retained its cabs as it was intended to become a motor car at the end of the trial.

The existing doors were retained and modified for air and electric operation using equipment from GD Peters. Through piping was fitted to allow 275s brakes to be controlled from 276. Internally Panax laminates were used for the side panels. Externally they were painted in an all-cream livery (save for a thin green beading strip below the windows). The new domes bore an illuminated legend above the blinds displaying 'LIMITED STOP' at one end and 'PROGRESS TWIN CAR' at the other. The cars were connected using a Willison automatic coupling from the English Steel Corporation of Sheffield, while batteries were fitted to each car for the bells and doors. Battery operated horns were fitted to the cab roofs - quite a contrast to the normal Blackpool air whistles.

Late in the evening of Saturday 18th January 1958 as the tram service wound down, 276 led 275 out of the depot and down Lytham Road onto the Promenade for the first time, to be greeted by a gale and waves breaking over the seafront. Joe Franklin, with his engineering managers and staff, were on board along with two councillors who rode the cars to Fleetwood. A ministry official inspected the set informally in February, ahead of formal sanctioning which took place not long after - the key to the scheme was undoubtedly the through braking and interlocking between the doors and controllers satisfying the safety requirements of the inspectorate. On 9th April the set was formally launched and ran from Talbot Square to Fleetwood and back. The Mayor of Blackpool drove it as far as Norbreck with another councillor and Franklin sharing the driving for the rest of the trip. No less than six councillors drove on the way back!

The pioneer Twin set 276+275 head towards Norbreck in this 1960 shot. (Brian Turner)

The Trade Union was busy negotiating extra pay for drivers and this prevented conventional service use - although it did happen by slight of hand. To occupy the cars a new Coastal Tour was devised - basically a full round trip picking up at Talbot Square, Central Station, Pleasure Beach and Starr Gate - and the set duly entered service on 24th May with a three shilling fare charged. The tour continued into the mid-1960s on an occasional basis only. Once the union was satisfied regarding wages, 276+275 were used on conventional service duties, although difficulties were experienced. The set could only turn around at the four loops, but could not fit on to most of the Tramroad stops, as the paved area was only long enough for one car at a time. A new service was devised which called at limited stops, hence the 'LIMITED STOP' sign at the end of 276. Those stops on the Promenade were identified by stripes on the pole and an infilled polo stop sign, while the handful on the Tramroad had extended paved areas. There was no published timetable - the set and its later sisters generally ran as specials.

This different service caused confusion as the trams were not distinctive enough. Attempts were made to counter this by listing some stops on the ends and sides of the prototype set, but eventually limited stop operation was abandoned and in the quite rare event that passengers wanted to alight from both halves at an unmodified Tramroad stop, the tram would have to pull up twice. When one man cars were introduced in 1972 they had a distinctive new livery to signify a different tram type. Had this and a published timetable been implemented for the limited stop Twin Cars, then perhaps the service could have been more successful. However as no time advantage was offered over the stopping cars (as the Twin Cars could not overtake) it was all rather pointless. Despite all this the trial operation was deemed to be successful enough to place an order for ten new trailers. Curiously, Franklin recommended converting 10 more Railcoaches - and re-equipping 275 - to make 12 motor cars, presumably for added flexibility as he perceived that trailers would require less maintenance downtime than motors. However the extra two cars were never remodelled and just 8 more conversions took place. The production cars differed from the initial pair in many ways, yet neither 275 nor 276 were modified to match. They retained their sunshine roofs for many years, and today still have their original platform doors and non-standard interiors.

Left: *During its brief period as a trailer, 275 kept its driving cabs but was largely shorn of equipment. All that is visible is the handbrake, required for securing the car in an emergency. (Brian Turner)*

Right: *276 shows off its clean lines at Pleasure Beach. Note the destination already set for its next trip, the roof mounted horns and the strings of lights characteristic of Railcoaches but less so of Twin Cars. 276 retained many Railcoach features including angled skirt panels, recessed windows, sliding roof and original platform doors. T3 is in tow. (TLP)*

TWIN CAR STOPS

Starr Gate
Jubilee
Harrowside
Southdown
Star Hotel
Pleasure Beach
South Pier
Waterloo Road
St Chads Road
Manchester Square
Central Pier
Central Station
Victoria Street
Talbot Square
Pleasant Street
Wilton Parade
Derby Baths
Gynn Square
Cliffs
Cabin
Miners Home
Bispham
Norbreck
Little Bispham
Anchorsholme
Cleveleys
Thornton Gate
Rossall Beach
Rossall School
Rossall Square
Broadwater
Lingfield Road
Stanley Road
Ash Street
Victoria Street
Fleetwood Ferry

THE MOTOR CARS

Once the order for the trailers had been placed, work could commence on converting the first of the Railcoaches into towing cars. October 1959 saw 277 enter the works, followed at the end of the month by 272. 277 beat its sister out of the works by two months - its remodelling was completed in late June, shortly before the arrival of the first trailer. The conversions had four stages: Firstly the cars were stripped to shells in the Fitting Shop including the removal of all electrical equipment and cab ends. Secondly, in the Body Shop, the trucks were removed for overhaul and work began on the roofs, the roof windows and the framework for the new fibreglass ends. New aluminium panelling was fitted, together with glazing, doors and new interiors. Once the trucks were returned the third stage involved a return to the Fitting Shop where the trucks and wiring were connected followed by stage 4, which was a full repaint in the Paint Shop.

In the intervening two years between the work on 276 and 277, the lengthy procedure of removing sliding roofs from the tram fleet (not completed until 1980) had begun. 277 was thus rebuilt with a fixed roof and rubber-mounted roof windows flush with the panelling. A less noticeable change was the replacement of the traditional angled panels either side of the entrance with curved ones - Coronation style. The doors were replaced by Metro Cammell examples similar to those on the trailers - differing from 275+276 which retained Railcoach doors, albeit power operated. The destination blinds were a then-unique yellow on black design to signify limited stop operation. Furthermore the fixed glass above the blind at one end displayed the legend 'Limited Stop' in yellow lettering on a black background and 'Progress Twin Car' in yellow on green at the other end. The trailers generally showed 'Progress Twin Car' and this was later adopted for all 20 vehicles. In 1960/61 removable boards were fitted to the front lower panels listing some of the main stops.

Other variations concerned the interiors. The turquoise laminated plastic side panels used on the prototypes were replaced by wood effect ones which complemented the lightly stained wooden window frames and the panelling above. Less graceful was the checker plate aluminium which covered the platform bulkheads. The original concealed lighting was retained, despite this having been removed on 276.

277 and trailer T1 made their first outing on 17th July 1960 with a test run to Fleetwood. When T2 arrived the following month it was paired with 276, although prototype trailer 275 often deputised for either T1 or T2. The next motor car, 272, emerged from the Paint Shop in September 1960 and quickly entered service with the newly delivered T3. Railcoaches 280 and 281 had been stored at Marton during the winter and the

The towing cars were rebuilt from 1935 English Electric Railcoaches. A sister car still largely in original condition passes Royal Oak junction shortly before the closure of the Lytham Road route in October 1961. (Brian Turner)

latter entered the works in April 1960, followed by 280 in May. 279 was then damaged in an accident with a lorry, so entered the works in June. For a few days prior to 277s completion 272, 277, 279, 280 and 281 were all under conversion. 281 was the next to be completed in November 1960 and was replaced in the works by the prototype trailer 275 for motorisation.

All four completed motor cars saw solo use on the Lytham Road route during winter 1960/61, indeed this was 281s first use, having just missed the end of the season. All ten trailers had arrived by the end of January 1961 but the towing car conversion programme had only produced six cars, even with the completion of 275 and 280 at Easter. Trailer use recommenced over the holiday with 276+T1, 277+T2, 272+T3 and 280+T5 in service. 279 was nearing completion of its overhaul whilst those on 273 and 278 were in progress, their having entered the works in January and February respectively. The tenth car - 274 - was still in service in original condition.

By Whit 272, 275, 276, 277, 279, 280 and 281 were in service paired with their corresponding trailers (T2, T5, T6, T7, T9, T10 and T1), starting a practice which has continued with little or no variation since. 273 was completed in early June followed by 278 in July. 274 finally entered the works in August and was finished in May 1962, some time after the rest of the batch. T4, which had been delivered in October 1960, had seen little recorded use by this time, although it is believed to have appeared briefly when still a new arrival.

Above: The new partly fibreglass front end has been fitted to 280 in this September 1960 shot. The car alongside is probably 281 which was completed shortly before 280.

Left: The rebuilding process started by stripping the body of the Railcoach to a shell. Car 280 is shown with its cab ends and interior removed.

Page 6: The subject and its creator: General Manager Joe Franklin walks past the front of the first production Twin set 277 and T1 on the day of its launch. Ironically, 274, still as a Railcoach, is on the adjacent track! (Brian Turner x 3)

BLACKPOOL

BLACKPOOL CORP
LIMITED

| JUBILEE | SOUTHDOWN | PLEASURE BEACH | WATERLOO ROAD | MANCHESTER SQUARE COLISEUM BUS STATION | CENTRAL STATION | NORTH PIER TALBOT SQUARE | WILTON PARADE | GYNN SQ |

STARR GATE — HARROWSIDE — STAR HOTEL — SOUTH PIER OPEN AIR BATHS — ST CHADS ROAD — CENTRAL PIER — VICTORIA STREET — PLEASANT STREET — WARLEY ROAD DERBY BATHS

THE TRAILER CARS

Of the £9000 cost of each set, £7680 was spent on the trailer. Bodies were built by Metro-Cammell, Blackpool's favoured bus body builder, as there was no tram-building capacity in the UK by this time. The trailers (at 43ft 10in) were longer than the motor cars (40ft 9in). This resulted in a five window saloon compared to four windows on the motor cars. 66 seats were fitted - two bench seats for five passengers each and the remainder a modern version of the traditional swing-over seats. Naturally they were designed to resemble the motor cars and featured rubber-mounted roof windows and a similar body line. The curved radius saloon windows were also rubber-mounted and included four half-drop windows on each side. The most prominent external differences were the road lights (tail lights only - no headlights) and the end windows which had opening top lights. The trucks, built by Maley & Taunton at £2797 per pair, incorporated rubber suspension.

The interior finish included imitation-wood lower panels and mushroom coloured painted metal window surrounds and coves similar to those found on Blackpool's buses. Bulb lighting was adopted, concealed behind glass covers which were fitted between the roof windows and the decorative alhambrinal ceilings. The roof windows were divided from the saloon windows by a plastic strip into which was inserted a map showing the points served by the limited stop service.

With no cabs, equipment was hidden in a number of places. The conductor had access to an emergency brake on the platform and could control the interior lights. A brake wheel was hidden under each bench seat with a hatch to access the handle, and other switches and equipment were also kept here.

T1, the first trailer, was delivered on 16th July 1960. Transported by rail from Metro-Cammell to Bolton, it was transhipped to a road vehicle and brought to Blackpool. Unloaded on track 16, it was immediately prepared for its first journey, which took place the following day - a test run to Fleetwood with the first production towing car (277). T1 was officially handed over by Metro-Cammell on 19th July before a run (again with 277) to Little Bispham. The party alighted at the Imperial Hotel on their return for a celebratory lunch. It is believed that T1 then entered service, following which T2 arrived on 21st July and entered service immediately. T3 followed on 6th September. Only three motor cars were available (272/276/277) and generally these ran with T1, T2 and T3 (in no order) but the derailment of seven day old T3 and a minor collision for T2 saw 275 stand in during October. T4 arrived on 13th October and presumably saw service straight away for the last few weeks of the season. Certainly on the last day of October the three motor cars were paired with T1 (277), T2 (272) and T4 (276), leaving T3 and 275 standing alone. This was the day of T5s arrival and further deliveries continued during the winter: T6 arrived on 14th November; T7 on 29th November; T8 on 13th December; T9 on 3rd January 1961 and T10 on 23rd January.

As noted earlier T1, T2, T3 and T5 were in use when trailer operation resumed at Easter 1961 - this was T5s first duty. T6, T7, T9 and T10 were all in use at Whit, coupled with their numeric equivalents in the motor car series (276/277/279/280). T8 is believed to have made its debut with 278 in July but it is understood that T4 did not operate during 1961, as its motor car, 274, was not completed until May 1962. T6 to T10 seem to have only operated with motor cars 276 to 280, although the first five trailers were paired with any available motor (272/276/277/280) before Whit 1961.

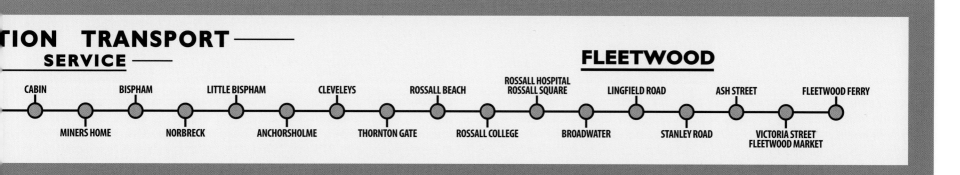

Above: *Trailer T1 arrived at 08.50 on 16th July 1960 and by 09.40 was placed on these jacks. Its trucks were positioned underneath soon afterwards and the lowering process is in progress in this image. The whole procedure was completed by 12.10 and Railcoach 211 shunted the trailer into the compound. (Brian Turner)*

Opposite: *1960 saw the most fluidity in the pairings of motor cars and trailers. This rare colour shot taken at Cleveleys in late 1960 shows 272 towing the prototype trailer 275. 272 had only emerged from the Paint Shop in September, while 275 was taken back in for conversion to a motor car in November. (TLP)*

When operating on the 'Limited Stop' service, wooden boards were hung on the front dash panel to highlight the stops served. The boards listed stops between South Pier and Norbreck - so could cover both Little Bispham and Fleetwood journeys, and varied by direction.

Top: 276 is pictured passing Central Pier with a journey to Fleetwood, carrying the boards for a southbound journey!

Below: 278 (with T8) at Fleetwood is showing northbound boards - but on the wrong sides! (Vic Nutton x 2)

Above: T1 arrived somewhat battle scarred with one of its curved corner windows damaged. Metro-Cammell engineers fitted a replacement which promptly shattered! Few trams could have gone through three windows before turning a wheel. (Brian Turner)

Opposite: 280s driver has got it wrong too - it's operating south towards Pleasure Beach but with northbound boards! (TLP)

LIMITED STOP

PLEASURE BEACH
VIA PROMENADE

SOUTH PIER	PLEASANT ST.
WATERLOO RD.	WILTON PARADE
ST CHADS RD.	WARLEY RD.
MANCHESTER SQ.	GYNN SQ.
CENTRAL PIER	CLIFFS
CENTRAL STN.	CABIN
VICTORIA ST.	MINERS' HOME
TALBOT SQ.	BISPHAM
COCKER SQ.	NORBRECK

280

Above: *Pleasure Beach to Little Bispham is a journey with which Twin Cars are very familiar. In their early life when the trailers had no driving cabs they were two of their few suitable termini. 278+T8 head south, passing 277+T7 at Bispham in 1967. Note the tape to cover the legend above the destination - perhaps disguising the former 'LIMITED STOP' designation.*

Opposite: *As summer beasts, Twin Cars rarely experience the snow, not that snow often falls on Blackpool. This shot on New Year's Day 1962 shows towing car 273 in use as a solo Railcoach heading for Starr Gate on service route 80. (Brian Turner x 2)*

TURNING TRIANGLE

Although intended to be flexible, in practice the Twin sets were rarely uncoupled. At the depot this meant that the sets had to be turned each day before service. By good fortune a turning triangle existed, giving access to Blundell Street from the track fan and Hopton Road.

Adjacent to the depot was the busy Coliseum coach station. On busy days the turning of the trams could be rather a fraught process, as these shots from the summer of 1966 illustrate.

Above: In the distance the previous set completes the manoeuvre and heads off towards the Promenade. Meanwhile T8 awaits clearance to take its turn.

Left: 278 then pushes its trailer alongside the Fitting Shop and is mobbed by children, probably dashing for a coach which was using the Bus Yard as overspill parking from the Coliseum. No doubt the depot shunter has kept the crowd at bay, as 278s driver has a near 44ft long blind spot in front of the cab.

Above: On a much quieter day 276 pushes T6 onto Blundell Street against the Fitting Shop wall.

Right: 279 completes the move turning into Hopton Road. The conductor has just removed the bamboo pole from the trolley, having helped guide it through the overhead frogs. The Ribble "Gay Hostess" Atlantean in the background awaits another party of returning holidaymakers on the regular London express service. (Brian Turner x 4)

PERMANENT PAIRS

The trailers have always operated attached to one motor car for a complete duty. In Blackpool's traffic conditions it was impractical to operate them otherwise. The various connections between the cars would probably have caused problems if the trailers had been detached on the road, particularly as so many of the high-season tram drivers were, in fact, bus drivers doing an odd tram turn, and so many of the guards were students. Nor was it practical to leave the trailers in the depot during off-peak hours, as on the Continent, because of the highly variable traffic demand throughout the day, and also because road traffic at Manchester Square makes access to Rigby Road depot difficult.

So the Twin Cars were permanently coupled for each duty, and were therefore effectively single-ended. At first trailers were not attached to specific motor cars and several permutations were to be seen, but from 1961 the practice evolved of coupling each trailer to the motor car with the same final number. To even out wear, the motor car would occasionally be reversed.

It was the intention, when the trailers were ordered, that the motor cars would operate as single Railcoaches during the winter, and this was done spasmodically in the early years. They operated from Rigby Road depot, where the Twin Cars have always been based, mainly on Promenade service duties. During January and February 1961, four cars (272, 276, 277 and 281) also worked on Lytham Road. On 4th June 1961, 275 was hired for a private tour, visiting Squires Gate Lane, Station Road and Waterloo Road.

Then, during the winter of 1962/63, a very interesting composite Sunday duty operated which involved cars doing a Fleetwood - Starr Gate trip followed by a Fleetwood - North Station run. So the Twin Car motor cars also made an appearance on Dickson Road, in the last year of its use by trams.

The Transport Department was reluctant to use the motor cars singly to too great a degree because of the possibility of strain on the Willison coupler through uneven tyre wear between the motor car and the trailer. However this problem resolved itself with the reduction in route mileage since 1961. The winter services of 1960, calling for some 50 cars on four routes, gradually gave way to the 1965 winter timetable, requiring 16 cars at the most on the Promenade route only. The make-up of the fleet reflected this change of emphasis. Between 1960 and 1965 the fleet of 48-seat single-deckers had dwindled from 83 to 30, which was more than sufficient to meet all the off-season demands of the tramway.

By the time the full fleet was available for service in 1962, it was becoming increasingly apparent that the full potential of the Twin Cars could not be realised while they were restricted to four reversal points: Starr Gate and

Left: *281+T1 were the first set to be permanently coupled and also the first to gain this new 'half and half' livery. Despite appearances, T1 is leading in this shot, running wrong line at Little Bispham due to a derailed Boat Car on the southbound track. (Brian Turner)*

Above: *T1+281 were coupled together whilst still in the cream livery. Close inspection of the trailer cab shows the half-height bulkhead initially fitted to this car. It spent two seasons in this configuration prior to the 1965 conversion of sets 2 to 5. (Brian Turner Collection)*

Pleasure Beach in the south, Little Bispham and Fleetwood in the north. This meant a minimum run of some five miles, of which the last mile, from Bispham to Little Bispham was very unremunerative. Traffic past Bispham is generally bound for Cleveleys and beyond, and it became a familiar sight to see almost empty Twin Cars trailing up past Norbreck to Little Bispham to reverse, just as the Streamlined double deckers used to do in the 1950s on the Squires Gate - Little Bispham service.

Further south, the disadvantages of single-ended working were felt very forcibly by the inspectors who, during the season, controlled the traffic by ad hoc decisions governing the special cars on the road, which sometimes numbered more than fifty at the height of the season in the 1960s. To them the Twin Cars' lack of flexibility was a serious handicap.

The obvious answer lay in making the cars reversible, and the first steps towards this end came in 1962, when the Western Train took to the rails, reconstructed from first series Railcoach 209. Pantograph Car was 174 rebuilt as the trailer, using the spare set of Willison couplings intended for the two additional conversions which were never carried out. There was one important difference from the Twin Cars, which was that the open rear platform of 174 carried an English Electric DB1 controller which had seen service originally on the 10 - 21 class before they became Marton Vambacs. This controller was used to reverse the cars from Talbot Square to Rigby Road depot after Tours of Illuminations, and consequently operated only on the series and brake notches, driving the motor car 209. The controller has a claim to fame in that it performed the final tramway operation of the Marton route, returning from the opening event of the ABC Theatre on 31st May, 1963. For braking, the carriage was fitted with a handbrake, with a

Left: *Reversing at Cabin and then again at Talbot Square was unthinkable prior to the rebuilding of the trailers. Here T2 leads its motor car off the centre track at Cabin for the short journey back to Talbot Square on 6th August 1966.*

Right: *Bispham was now a feasible turning point for the permanently coupled Twin Cars. Here T4s driver begins to draw the set forward onto the middle line. A small crowd of northbound passengers diligently obey the 'Queue Other Side' instruction. (Brian Turner x 2)*

base under the long seat on the platform, and a traditional upright brake handle which was stowed away against the bulkhead when not in use. Prudently the Transport Department prohibited inquisitive children from riding on the rear platform of the trailer.

The reversing equipment on the Western Train was soon considered rather primitive in comparison with the compact battery-operated Allen West remote controllers and air brakes of H.M.S. Blackpool and the Hovertram, but it proved to the Department that it was perfectly feasible to operate Twin Cars with the trailer leading. The next step was to experiment with an actual set and 281+T1 emerged from the works, semi-permanently coupled and with a cab at each end. Driving from the trailer called for rather careful judgment of section gaps, as the trolley head was about ninety feet behind the driver, the air brakes took rather longer to release than on a normal car, and the acceleration was not quite as good when the trailer was leading. T1 was an ideal car for the tram enthusiast, as it was fitted with only a waist-high partition behind the driver, which gave the car rather a continental air.

Two seasons' experience with 281+T1 in this form convinced the Department that this was the answer to the inflexibility of the Twin Cars. For the 1965 season four further sets were rebuilt for double-ended operation, numbers 272+T2, 273+T3, 274+T4 and 275+T5. Immediately after the end of the 1964 season, work began and while 272+T2 were in the works, 281+T1 were repainted into the now standard half green and half cream livery. The four modified sets followed on completion, leaving the five unrebuilt sets in their original cream.

The concept of trailer-first operation was believed to be new on a British tramway, although not by any means elsewhere. Among systems known to have operated on the same principle are the NZH in Holland, Paris, Marseilles, Alexandria, Cologne, the OEG Mannheim-Heidelberg, Rome-Fiuggi, Milan interurbans, Stockholm route 12 and Lidingo. All of these have worked on one variation or another, but you would certainly have to go a long way to see an exact parallel of the Blackpool operation of a trailer without collecting apparatus being propelled by a trolley-equipped power car.

"You may have to modify them in thirty years or so" said Major Cole of Metro-Cammell when the first trailer was officially handed over in 1960, and certainly the trailers were not built with any intention of simple rebuilding, any more than Metro-Cammell's buses were. They were built to withstand normal service stresses and no more, and it was therefore vital that the rebuilding be carried out with the greatest care in order not to affect the strength of the cars. Basically the rebuilding involved transferring the equipment from the No. 2 end of the power car to the No. 1 end of the trailer. The No. 1 end of

the cars contained the majority of switchgear and ancillary equipment, and it was obviously preferable to have the driving positions at that end.

The trailers were accordingly given driver's cabs, with full-size partitions in place of the waist-high panelling of the prototype 281+T1. The partitions were constructed from timber, panelled with aluminium, and their positioning presented various problems. Considerations of space for, on the one hand, the driver, and on the other, the passengers dictated that the partition be placed between the first two window pillars. This meant that the sides of the partition do not fit flush against the sides of the car, and, because of the continuous rows of lights in the roof, the partition cannot extend fully to the roof, so as to allow access to the light fittings. Only the centre portion of the partition, which contains the driver's door, extends to the roof, and even here, the absence of roof framework precludes a rigid attachment. The

driver sits on a seat mounted on a tubular column, and to reduce glare the section of saloon lighting within the new cab was painted black. The circuit breaker is fitted at waist level on the partition. The driver's cab at the No. 2 end of the motor car was removed, the interior panelled, and the floor built up to the level of the saloon, ready for the fitting of the long five-passenger bench seat from the end of the trailer. This increased the capacity of the motor car to 53.

The equipment removed from the motor car was then installed in the cab of the trailer. This was by no means as easy as it sounds, for the nature of the trailer's construction did not allow for the placing of heavy equipment including Z6 controllers right at the end of the car. The works solved this by building a special strengthening sub-frame under the end of the trailer's frame to spread the load without distortion, and this, together with the

shape of the original frame, meant fitting the controller parallel with the side of the car, and also placing the standard vertical wheel handbrake, which replaced the under-seat wheel, almost square. The air brake and various gauges were also fitted in the trailer's cab.

An interesting part of the conversion was the fitting of the various floor controls into the trailer. The lifeguard mechanism and tray were transferred from the motor car and linked up with the trailer's metal gates, and the normal horn button was fixed into the floor. Instead of the two-tone electric horns mounted on the roofs of the power cars, the trailers were fitted with old style air-operated under-floor hooters. It was felt that the familiar Blackpool hooter is a more effective warning than the two-tone horns which sound very "un-tram-like".

For ingenuity, though, the sanding gear took the prize, for the driver needed to be able to operate the sanders in front of the wheels of the motor car fifty feet behind him, and to achieve this mechanically would have been extremely difficult. Consequently the works devised the first remote control sanding gear on a British tram. The floor button in the trailer was electrically connected to a solenoid in each of the sanders in the motor car. A coil, when energised by depressing the button, lifts the solenoid, which releases the sand. The coils used in this apparatus were originally used as clutch coils in the Marton Vambacs - they engaged and disengaged the revolving contact arm in the control equipment mounted below the trolley tower.

Although there was at the time no thought of rebuilding the cars, the order for the trailer cars specified that the Auster opening windscreen should be the same size as the standard Blackpool opening windscreen, and this has meant that a trailer windscreen could simply be exchanged for the opening windscreen of a motor car. As far as is known, this is the only instance of deliberate interchangeability of equipment on the cars. Against the new partition were fitted two fixed seats, facing the centre of the car, in place of the end two swing-over seats, and with the loss of the five passenger seats, the seating capacity of the trailers was now 61, making a 53/61 combination instead of 48/66, and balancing the work of the guards rather better than before. Six standing passengers were allowed on each car, making a total capacity of 126.

Perhaps the most complex part of the rebuilding involved the wiring. The 550v DC power supply had to be taken the full length of the set to the trailer's controller, and this was done by a total of 18 cables, comprising eight motor leads, four to each motor, eight resistance leads, one earth and one trolley connection. These cables are carried from the motor car to the trailer through two sets of special plugs and sockets, each with nine

connections, which are mounted on the dash panel, if one can call it that, of the motor car. The cables are attached to the plugs and are taken through the dash panel of the trailer, and thence to the controller. The idea behind these connections is that if the cars should break apart in service, then the power cables would simply be pulled out of their sockets with no danger of live 550v cables being exposed. They also provide a simple means of separation in the depot. Several other adjustments had to be made to the 24v circuits for bells, doors, etc., and to the air piping under the trailer.

As far as external body alterations are concerned, the most obvious was the removal of the air-hosing and Willison couplings from the ends of the trams. The motor cars retained part of the coupling housing, painted cream in the case of 281 and green on the others, and the swept down fibreglass side wings, but in the case of the trailers, both were removed. In their place a metal fender with an emergency towing device was welded across the front of the car, extending some way round the sides, which gave the trailers a distinctive, if rather blunt, end appearance. The headlights from the motor cars were transferred to the trailers, which previously had tail lights only, and all the light fittings in the centre of the sets were removed, as were the indicator blinds, although behind the green-painted glass the bulbs remained intact, being part of the lighting circuit.

Converting these sets to permanently coupled units obviously involved some careful programming. The first stage was for the motor cars to enter the Fitting Shop, where all electrical and mechanical equipment was removed. This done, the cars were towed round to the Body Shop to make room for the trailers. The ease of access between the Body Shop and Fitting Shop allowed much of the transfer of body fittings to be effected at this stage. There is not a great deal of dismantling to be done on the trailers; the old handbrake is one item which is removed in the Fitting Shop.

When the body alterations to the power cars were complete, they were moved next door to the Paint Shop, and the trailers replaced them in the Body Shop for body alterations. From there the trailers returned to the Fitting Shop for the adding of cables, controllers and brake valves, and then took the place of the motor cars in the Paint Shop. The motors, meanwhile, were stored in the running depot until the trailers were repainted, and then the two cars were coupled together in the depot. The last stage was for the complete units to be taken into the Electrical Compound in the depot for checking, greasing and finishing.

On re-entering service, the rebuilt double-ended sets operated basically on

a service between Pleasure Beach and Bispham, augmented by various other workings, including Harrowside - Cabin. Obviously their flexibility resulted in much more efficient use than in previous years. It was intended to resume the conversion with sets 6 to 10 but this was not possible until after the 1968 renumbering when the motor cars became 672 to 680 and 671 (ex-272 to 281) and the trailers 681 to 690 in order. 676+686 were permanently coupled between May and August 1969, then 677+687 followed during spring 1970. It seems that work on set 6 over-ran as when 676 emerged from the Paint Shop in August it was coupled to a still-cream 686 and they completed the season in differing liveries - the only permanently coupled set to do so. 686 eventually received green and cream in November 1969.

Completion dates:	
281+T1	October 1962
272+T2	December 1964
273+T3	January 1965
274+T4	February 1965
275+T5	April 1965
676+686	August 1969
677+687	July 1970

The remaining three sets were never treated and saw occasional use until 1972 when the trailers were withdrawn and the motor cars left to run solo. 678, 679 and 680 had been repainted in the half and half livery during winter 1970/71 but their trailers were left in cream until the following winter and only managed a few weeks in service so painted before withdrawal in September 1972. They were barely run in. Annual mileage would have been less than 10,000 and they barely achieved the equivalent of two years' mileage of a year-round car.

They were dumped at the back of the depot, 688 at the end of track 15 in the compound where it became a mess room, 689 settled on the other side of the partition on track 14, while 690 gathered dust at the back of track 1, hidden for many years behind a stack of new sleepers. In late 1980/early 1981, 689 and 690 were moved into Blundell Street depot and, surprisingly, were sold to GEC for £800 each in November 1981. They were transferred to Kearsley Power Station near Bolton where they were motorised and ran on the internal railway for testing driverless control systems. After storage at Trafford Park, both moved to the West Yorkshire Transport Museum in 1985, ostensibly for preservation but both were scrapped in 1989. 688 meanwhile was extracted from the back of the compound and moved into the doomed Blundell Street depot in May 1982, where it was broken up in

November. Its trucks went under 681 - possibly the only instance of a trailer truck swap. The seven permanently coupled sets settled into a regular, if infrequent use pattern. They generally entered service in July and ran until the end of October. Use was most common on Tuesdays to help take the crowds to Fleetwood market and on busy Illumination evenings - their roof windows and high capacity made them popular for viewing the lights.

Through the 1970s little or nothing remarkable happened to the Twin Cars:

only 674+684 were repainted (in 1973) while 671, 672, 673 and 675 merely received green coloured towers instead of orange ones. Various touch-ups saw lower panel repaints for 673 and 677 and these - like 674 - received black fleet numbers as did 672 and 675. 671 and 676 retained their 1960s gold numbers. There were a few accidents involving the Twin Cars. T2 had a crushed cab in 1967, 684 had minor damage in 1975 while 673 was involved in a collision with 616 in July 1970 which led to the Railcoach becoming the first OMO car.

275 and 276 continued to stand out from their sisters as they retained their recessed roof windows, sliding sunshine roofs, Railcoach doors and angled centre skirt panels. Only 272 to 275 and 281 carried this livery, with 280 receiving an orange tower on its original cream livery by 1966! By the time of their next repaint, the cars had been renumbered and 676 emerged in August 1969 as one of the first with a green trolley tower. 677 to 680 followed and by 1973, 671 to 675 had also received green towers. On a fine sunny day the arm of a passenger points out of the first opening window of 675 as the trams pass Foxhall. The destination blind lettering is very square looking, complete with a small 'VIA'. (TLP)

Opposite: *The 1960s saw the adoption of a very simple half green and half cream livery embellished by a vivid orange trolley tower. The reason for this is lost in the mists of time, the less charitable observers suggesting it was chosen to disguise the rust. This livery made its first appearance on the Twin Cars in the 1965 season after 272+T2 to 275+T5 had been permanently coupled. Trailer T4 leads its motor into Talbot Square. (TLP)*

Above: *672 leads 682 onto Pleasure Beach loop in a familiar scene enlivened by the vivid yellow trousers worn by the passer by. Not for the first time two following cars have caught up with the Twin and the Brush Car driver is probably mightily relieved to have a clear road ahead to Starr Gate. (TLP)*

Right: In the same location as page 28, 274+T4 have become 674+684 and had received a full repaint into green and cream with green tower in October 1973. A new driver received training on the foibles of the Twin Car in this late 1970s scene as 633 heads for Fleetwood. Sadly 'Progress' has seen the ornate Prudential Building in the background replaced by a plainer brick building. (TLP)

Left: In 1985, 685 was one of a few scruffy looking trailers which had gone 20 years without a lick of paint. By contrast, 675, repainted in 1980, looks fine. Although the length difference was slight, 685 somewhat dominates its sister here almost to the point where the cars look like they are a different height, width and gauge! This is Manchester Square.

Opposite: Spot the conductor. Turning a trolley on a Twin Car was a challenging experience, as the elastic barriers prevented the conductor from stepping between the cars to get the perfect alignment. This one has managed though. Talbot Square, summer 1985. (Philip Higgs x 2)

Above: *By the end of the 1980s, the majority of the Twin Cars were in an appalling external condition, as clearly seen here on 671+681 at Pleasure Beach. With the crudely applied Blackpool Transport vinyls stuck over painted-out former BCT crests, some would say this was the lowest ebb, condition wise, for these cars. Closer observation shows a handful of new panels at the end of of 681, in a whiter shade of cream to the rest of the car.*

Opposite: *Apologies for another image of the beaten and worn 675+685 of 1989, pictured at Little Bispham. Despite not working any kind of 'CIRCULAR' tour for some decades, 685 still retained this destination on its blind and thanks to a friendly conductor, it was specially displayed for the camera on this occasion. 675 also sports a fully painted side roof advert for 'Professor Peabodys'. (Nick Meskell x 2)*

THE LOST TRAILERS

From 1965 the fleet was split with Sets 1 to 5 as permanently coupled double-ended units in half green and half cream and Sets 6 to 10 retaining their original livery and single ended configuration. With Sets 6 and 7 permanently coupled in 1969/70, this left T8 to T10 (688 to 690) as the only trailers in original condition. Their usage declined and remarkably they were withdrawn in 1972 after just twelve seasons of service.

Above: Little Bispham was one of their two northern termini and at Easter 1967 T9 - led as usual by 279 - sits on the loop awaiting a slot south - probably to Pleasure Beach.

Below: In 1968, complete with new numbers, 688 has just entered the loop and collected its conductor while 680+690 take the hint and depart south for Pleasure Beach. In the distance Engineering Car 753 sits on the little-used northbound exit spur. (Brian Turner x 2).

For the 1971 season, trailers 688 to 690 retained their original cream livery despite their motor counterparts having received the standard green and cream livery. In this amazingly well timed image at Norbreck, 679+689 pass 680+690 with both sets sporting the mixed livery. The guard of 690 seems eager to finish and has already set the destination blind for Manchester Square well ahead of its terminus at Little Bispham. (Brian Turner).

Right: *This trio spent almost as long in store as they did in the operating fleet. Visitors to the depot during the 1970s saw these cars become increasingly woebegone. By 1979, the unloved and dusty 689 is sandwiched between Open Boat 603 - which had returned the previous year from a visit to the USA, and Brush 636 - the accident damaged cab of which is just visible on the right of the photo. (Brian Turner)*

Left: *The fleet renumbering of 1968 took several weeks to complete and it was quite common to see trams of the same batch in service with original or new numbers. Perhaps the most extreme example was set 9, pictured here on 11th May 1968. On the left T9 had received its new number (689) yet its partner retained 279. Modern Tramway reported that set 2 ran for driver training as 272+682, suggesting that the more complex renumbering of the trailers preceded the simpler change to the motors. (Brian Turner)*

678 TO 680

In contrast to their trailers, 678, 679 and 680 had gone from under-utilised motor cars to the workhorses of the fleet. With the withdrawal of several Railcoaches for conversion into OMO cars, they were fitted with heaters as replacements and regularly operated on the winter service from 1970/71. Once all 13 OMO cars were in service the appearance of crew cars out of season became much rarer. More often than not those which did appear were 678, 679 or 680, particularly on route learning duties for new drivers, when they would substitute for One Man cars. All three were repainted in winter 1970/71 and again three years later.

678 achieved a claim to fame in 1975 when it became the first passenger car to operate with a pantograph for over 40 years. After alignment tests using Overhead Car 754 with a single arm Brecknell Willis pantograph, the collector was transferred onto 678 which entered service so equipped in July. Initially only the overhead from Starr Gate to Little Bispham was realigned, so 678 was restricted to this section. The full line was completed by January and 678 was joined by OMO 5 but then lost its pantograph, probably to car 13, in May 1976.

In July 1978, 678 received cab damage in a collision with OMO 3 at Starr Hotel and spent much of the rest of the year under repair and was then repainted as a result. Meanwhile 679 is believed to have missed most of 1977 with truck problems. It was reported out of use in September 1976 after derailments and was back in use in April 1978 "after a lengthy layoff".

The next to see works attention was 678, which entered the Body Shop for an overhaul in March 1984. It returned to use in early June resplendent in a revised livery pioneered on Brush Cars 622 and 637. The main body was off-white with a green roof and waistband which dipped under the windscreen. In April 1985, 679 and 680 entered the works for similar treatment and were outshopped in July. Around this time 679 was fitted with a pantograph (the first of the type to receive the new standard diamond pantographs). 678 and 680 were similarly equipped in 1988.

Along with 674+684, 679 featured in the centenary cavalcade on 29th September 1985. During 1986/87, all three cars were fitted with ex-OMO bogies with Metalastik suspension following the withdrawal of OMO cars 2, 3, 4 and 7. In March 1987, 679 was the first to receive an all-over advert, and this was for Associated British Ports to promote their Fleetwood to Isle of Man 'Funboat'. A year later 678 was repainted for 'Camelot'. This left just 680 in the 1980s livery, although all was not well with the car and an electrical failure saw the car withdrawn in October 1989.

1975 saw serious experimentation with pantograph operation. 678 was the first passenger car used for in-service tests of the Brecknell Willis single arm design. It ran from July 1975 to May 1976 restricted to the Starr Gate to Little Bispham section, as the overhead wire north of there had not been made compatible. (TLP)

April 1990 saw the car stripped in the Body Shop for an assessment. Major underframe and body work was needed and the car returned to store. Finally in July 1991 the remaining panels and wiring were removed and the shell put in the Fitting Shop for underframe repairs. The body frame was remedied and new sections inserted as required. The roof windows were removed and side windows replaced by flush-mounted units from OMO cars including hopper vents. The refurbished interior featured green aluminium side panels, darvic roof panels, wooden window frames and former Routemaster bus seats. The bulb lighting was concealed in units mounted in the centre of the roof (the only car so treated) and on completion it was repainted into the then latest fleet livery of green roof and skirt with cream body panels, although 680 was the first to receive matt black window surrounds. The power doors were replaced by new lightweight hand operated two piece doors as used on Balloon Cars. New windscreens had been fabricated with a separate upper section and a lower opening portion which only opened to

around 20 degrees rather than the right angle achieved by the old units. 680 was also the first crew car to receive a screen wash facility.

The new 680 entered service in April 1992. Meanwhile 679 had been found to need repairs, although not to the extent of 680. In April 1991 some panels were removed for replacement and an inspection revealed that underframe repairs were required. It was quickly moved to the Fitting Shop and the work was carried out. Back in the Body Shop a new floor with non-slip dimplex covering (as also fitted to 680) was laid and the opportunity was taken to remove the batteries and power operation from the doors. A set of ex-West Midlands Fleetline bus seats were fitted, which had been previously used for a while in 637. After a repaint in a revised 'Funboat' livery, 679 returned to service in June 1991, retaining its roof windows and half-drop openers.

The advert liveries continued to change. 678 received a scheme for 'North West Auto Trader' in May 1990 then returned to fleet livery in February 1993 (when it lost its batteries and power doors). This was to be fairly brief as in April 1995 it was painted into a design for the 'Little and Large Show' at the Blackpool Pleasure Beach Paradise Room. New windscreens were fitted similar to 680s. In February 1997 its half-drop windows were replaced by ex-OMO hopper units and the car ran in blue undercoat until it received a repaint in September 1997 into the first of two 'Royal British Legion' adverts (the second was painted in February 2000). 678s final advertising livery was for Radio Wave, as applied in 2004. 678 today retains swing over seating and is the most original of the trio. It lost its heaters -

Left: *680 was the only one of the trio to receive a major overhaul and returned to use in 1992 completely rebuilt, without roof windows and with flush-mounted glazing from withdrawn OMO cars. Here it leaves Little Bispham loop by the north spur during trackwork.*

Opposite: *By contrast 680 heads through the melting snow on this winter service duty in March 1980. (Brian Turner x2)*

and its status as a winter car - in 1993, although it operated on Saturdays during winter 2005/06 before withdrawal at the end of 2006 on the expiry of its advert.

Meanwhile 679 lost its 'Funboat' advert in July 1994 and gained an attractive scheme for 'Mecca Bingo', let down by the fitting of two large fibreglass bears to the cab roofs! New windscreens were fitted at the same time. In June 1995 it received another scheme, this time for 'Seagull Coaches', and carried this until the end of the 1998 season. It was soon admitted to the works for panelling repairs and had all its side windows replaced by ex-OMO car units, flush- mounted and with hopper vents. A replacement trolley tower and base were fitted, although the car was not repainted until June 1999. For the first time since 1987 it returned to fleet livery, although it differed from 680 as the green skirt was omitted. In February 2004, 679 was repainted into the attractive 1980s livery as part of a programme to recreate past liveries for the 70th Anniversary of the English Electric fleet. 679 was the last of the trio to retain heaters and saw regular winter weekend use until November 2004 when it was mothballed as part of the infamous fleet reduction of winter 2004/05. In October 2008 it was bought by the Lancastrian Transport Trust for restoration as a Railcoach and had a farewell run in November - the last recorded use for one of this trio.

Left: *A rather tired and dirty looking 678 in it's 'Auto Trader' advert is pictured at Pleasure Beach in 1992. The tram was on a late running journey from Fleetwood to Starr Gate, terminating here. (Nick Meskell)*

Opposite: *678 does a credible impression of a Twin Car again with either 679 or 680 behind at Talbot Square on 1st September 1986. This livery did not feature on many single deckers. (Brian Turner)*

Left: In February 2000 an attractive new half-red and half-blue livery was adopted for 678, bearing a strong resemblance to the 'Mecca Bingo' scheme carried by 679 in 1994. Looking truly wonderful, pictured in the morning sunshine outside the North Euston hotel in Fleetwood, the tram really was a special car for many people, retaining its delightful wooden interiors and a full set of swing-over seats. (James Millington)

678 was used to promote the Royal British Legion Poppy Appeal from 1997 to 2003. It made regular appearances on the timetabled service on Remembrance Sunday over the years.

Opposite: The initial livery was red, white and blue and for a while it promoted the Legion's scratchcard. This was removed in April 1998 and replaced by a Spice Girls promotion! Note the new home-made windscreens fitted in 1995 and the ex-OMO hopper window units fitted in 1997. This is Cleveleys, with the old waiting shelter.

Right: Perhaps 678s most bizarre journey in modern times took place on 20th July 2003 when it was used to tow the Illuminated Western Train Locomotive, 733, to Fleetwood for display at the Tram Sunday event. The journey started at 07.00 and the unusual ensemble is seen here crossing at Anchorsholme. (James Millington x 2)

Contrasting images between 678s very first advert in 1988 compared to its very last, almost 20 years later. Not only is the style, design and method of painting very different two decades apart, the 678 of the 1980s looks so warm and welcoming compared to the almost demonic and what appears to be an ill conceived vinyl advert of the 2000s.

Above: 678s first all-over advert in 1988 was for 'Camelot Theme Park' as seen at Fleetwood Ferry. This tram uniquely featured a bright green visor at one end. (Nick Meskell)

Above right: Black trams are, thankfully, somewhat rare. 678 was so repainted in February 2004 ready for an all-over advert for 'Radio Wave'. This took a little while to finalise, so the jet black 678 returned to service brightened only by the green ex-Twin Car glass, dayglo destination, white numbers and the checker plate repair to the dash. With the Big Blue Brasserie in the background, the big black tram heads along the recently reflagged New South Promenade to Starr Gate.

Below right: By July, the side advert vinyls had been applied and the car saw increasing use, however the ends remained black for a while. The tram is just south of Little Bispham. (James Millington x 2)

Above: The first few months of 2005 saw the renewal of the pointwork at Manchester Square which provided access to the depot. Work was sufficiently complete by Easter to allow trams to operate through the junction, despite the lack of a top surface. 678 heads over the new pointwork on a short Pleasure Beach to North Pier trip. The tram was finally wearing the full correct version of the 'Radio Wave' livery. (Nick Meskell)

Below: During the relaying the tram service ran between Fleetwood and North Pier, however access was maintained to the depot by the rarely used Foxhall route via Princess Street and Blundell Street. As these workings ran without passengers, the Lancastrian Transport Trust arranged a charity running day using four cars - including 678 - shuttling between depot and Foxhall Square on 28th February. (Paul Turner)

Above: *Seagull Coaches was a small local coach operator - acquired by Fylde Borough Transport in 1989. Blackpool Transport bought Fylde in 1994 and the company came with it. In 1995, 679 was repainted in this two-tone blue scheme promoting Seagull Coaches excursions. The tram is pictured at Bispham working specials.*

Above right: *Almost a year to the day - 2nd July 1996 - a debranded 679 arrives at Pleasure Beach. This was perhaps a taster of what might have been had Fylde beaten the odds and taken over Blackpool Transport instead!*

Right: *Winter 1998/9 saw 679 overhauled. Earlier in the year it received a new tower and ex-OMO car windows, but unlike 678 the fixed units were replaced by flush-mounted glazing too. The car was outshopped in 1990s livery with black window surrounds but without the green skirt. This gave a somewhat unfinished look but did allow these vivid side panel adverts for Flares Nightclub to be applied.*
(James Millington x 3)

Above: In 2004 the 70th Anniversary of the Streamlined Fleet was celebrated in a September event. Several Balloons received heritage liveries and 679 was selected to represent the Railcoaches - albeit a heavily rebuilt one. It was decided to paint the car into the short-lived 1980s livery and here Engineering Car 754 tows a freshly painted 679 out of the Paint Shop on 12th February 2004.

Below: In its first incarnation, 679 only carried this scheme for the 1985 and 1986 seasons before receiving an all-over advert. Alas this version was no more long-lived as the car was withdrawn in November 2004. This image, taken on 22nd March 2004, shows the car on the last remaining operational section of the Lytham Road route, the short distance between the Promenade and Hopton Road. Although sporting a pantograph and yellow destination blind, the same 279 was a regular car along this stretch from 1935 until 1960, working the all-year service to the Airport. Incredibly, the tram made a brief return, running along most of the Lytham Road route on the back of a low loader on 25th April 2009 en-route from the Rigby Road depot to the premises of the Lancastrian Transport Trust at Brinwell Road.
(James Millington x 2)

Right: 680s first all-over advert was not applied until May 1995. The cream base may have been redolent of an earlier period in its life, but the livery for 'Scruffy Murphy's Irish Pub' was bland in the extreme and appeared somewhat unfinished. This is Pleasure Beach on 13th June 1995 with the tram having just entered the inner loop while working specials. The driver glances behind, looking for his conductor who would have just closed the points behind the tram.

Below: July 1996 saw the application of a more interesting scheme for 'Dillons Bookstore'. Pictured on 10th August 1996, the tram is at Manchester Square about to head along Lytham Road and to depot after a day of specials.

Below Right: The third scheme for 680 was this red and white based livery to mark 50 years of the 'Leonard Cheshire' disability care charity. The tram is at Tower. (James Millington x 3)

Left: Advert number four for 680 was a multi-coloured scheme for Central Pier - this was one of the last designs painted by the legendary signwriter Brian Hamer before his untimely death. Winter 2003/04 had seen the car totally repanelled, 12 years after its major overhaul, although the car did not return to service until August 2004. Along with its sisters 678 and 679, 680 retained the bulkhead mounted saloon heaters for many years, making it suitable for all year service. In winter 1999/2000, when Blackpool Transport reintroduced an all-year weekend Pleasure Beach - Cleveleys service, the three ex-Towing cars found themselves back on front line winter service, albeit only on Saturdays and Sundays. 678 was not used all that often as its heaters failed and were duly removed. 680 lasted a while longer until its heaters also failed and were taken out. This left 679 as the sole survivor and it retained working heaters up until its final day in service in 2004. (James Millington)

Right: 680s final all-over advert in 2006 was for the Merrie England Bar on North Pier in this all-over blue base. Pictured at Pleasure Beach on 27th August 2006, the tram is on specials, entering the outer loop. As can be seen in these five photos, the tram appears to have retained black and white destination blinds thoughout its lifetime but in fact the 'SANDCASTLE and PLEASURE BEACH' end as shown in the 'Scruffy Murphy's' and 'Merrie England' adverts is in fact a sun bleached yellow one gone white! (Nick Meskell)

1990s RENAISSANCE

After two decades of minimal attention, the start of the 1990s heralded a new era for the Twin Cars. Predating this, 674 was equipped with ex-OMO car bogies in February 1988, probably the pair removed from OMO 9 at the same time - these had been overhauled in 1985. The OMO bogies had been modified in the 1970s to use Metalastik rubber suspension instead of traditional leaf springs - the trailer car bogies having an earlier form of rubber suspension. These bogies were slightly higher than standard ones and the motor car became about 6" higher. As a result, 674+684 parted company a number of times once they coming back into use. Returning to January 1990 and 671+681 were split. Both received panel repairs in the compound and 671 was fitted with a pantograph base. 681 was repainted first, being replaced by 671 in the Paint Shop on February 2nd. It emerged three weeks later, matching 681 in the new fleet livery: cream with green roof, skirt and

doors - their first repaint for 26 years. Once the pantograph had been fitted and the set recoupled, 671+681 made a rare appearance at Easter on specials, although unfortunately this was curtailed when they split at Talbot Square. A more serious such occurrence happened in September 1990, which resulted in the rear panel of 671 being pulled out. Repairs were effected quickly, however.

Meanwhile the overhauls continued with 673+683 treated between April and June, then 675+685 done from June to August. For the rest of 1990 all seven sets were in use, three with new livery and pantographs and four in the old scheme with trolleys. In January 1991, 672+682 were split, 672 received ex-OMO car trucks and moved into the Body Shop where it was extensively repanelled before a repaint during May. 682 had been repainted during March and this pair was the first set to feature new Blackpool Transport and Tramway logos. They returned to service in July.

676+686 were split in May. 686 received panel repairs in August and a repaint in October. 676 needed more extensive work than the other motor cars, including the renewal of its platform underframe, and was repainted in August. Work then commenced on 686 and was completed in October. The set did not run in 1991 and returned to use in June 1992. Surprisingly 677 received a pantograph in June 1991 while retaining the old livery, leaving just 674 with a trolley. This spent the year as a last resort car and did not run until August. In early October, Set 4 entered the works, 674 receiving a pantograph and after a few weeks in the Body Shop it was given a repaint during November. Meanwhile 684 had been painted in October, so the set was recoupled once 674 emerged. Finally 677+687 were attended to from the end of November and after minor body repairs were repainted in late December/early January.

Left: *Similar but different. 673 shows the neater front end with the boxed-in tow pin box (as per 676 and 679) compared to the open version on 677. The latter has a deeper green skirt, offset fleet numbers and displays tramway logos. Note also the replacement windscreens on 673 compared to the originals on 677. Both cars are returning to depot after a day on specials - 677+687 are about to pull on to the centre track at Tower which has just been vacated by 673+683. (James Millington)*

Above: *674 was retrucked in December 1987 with a set of ex-OMO car trucks with rubber suspension. This rare shot shows it on the venerable body lift on track 11. Note also the short-lived brown and green BT logos and the somewhat pointless inner end fleet number. (Brian Turner)*

So for 1992 all seven sets had a uniform appearance in the new livery with pantographs. This made them more flexible, as conductors didn't need to struggle to turn a trolley between two cars. 672+682 missed most of 1993/94 with electrical problems. They received a low voltage inverter to replace their batteries and after teething problems during the brief period they ran in 1994, the set returned to full use in 1995.

In 1997, 674 received a new yellow on black destination blind (a throwback to the special blinds of the 1960s) but was later split from 684 for panel repairs and the fitting of a new windscreen (similar to 678 to 680). 684 also received the new windscreens and both were repainted in July/August.

On a less pleasant note there were two major accidents in 1997. Firstly in July Centenary Car 644 ran into the back of 681 at St. Chad's Road, wiping out the driving cab of the trailer. The following month a northbound 724 took a sudden diversion onto Little Bispham loop into the back of 682, because the points had not been changed back. Although the Balloon was repaired, the underlying damage was such that it was stripped for a major rebuild in 2000. 671+681 were stored but 682 was quickly separated from 672 and repaired in the Body Shop. A new-style windscreen was fitted and the tram was moved back to the depot. In June 1998 (eight months after leaving the Body Shop) 682 moved into the Paint Shop for a complete repaint. 672 was similarly treated after receiving a new windscreen and both gained the new yellow on black blinds. The recoupled set returned to service on 25th August 1998, five days short of the anniversary of the accident.

Many doubted that Set 1 would run again, such was the devastation to the trailer cab. Despite this, 681 moved into the Body Shop in April 1998 and the damaged end was stripped down to the bulkhead. It later moved to the Fitting Shop for the fabrication of a new cab underframe and returned to the Body Shop for the new cab frame and panelling. It was finally transferred to the Paint Shop in November for a full repaint. 671 had suffered minor damage and its inner end was repaired in May, also losing its opening window. It was fully repainted in July 1998 but had to await completion of 681. They were finally returned to service in June 1999, nearly two years after the accident.

The remaining sets 673+683, 675+685, 676+686 and 677+687 retained their 1990/91 paintwork, though Set 3 received new windscreens and 675 a new tower base. 676 missed the entire 2001 season awaiting a truck overhaul which finally took place in November with the fitting of a set of Metalastik suspension bogies - the third and final towing car so treated. During its accident repair 671 was fitted with an inverter joining 672, while 673 was so

treated in 1999 (when it got its new windscreen) and 677 received one in late 2001. 674, 675 and 676 had also been so fitted by 2002. The inverter powered the low voltage system, allowing the batteries to be removed.

Ironically, despite the permanent coupling in the mid-1960s and the pantograph fitting of the early 1990s, most Twin Car journeys ran from Pleasure Beach to Little Bispham or Fleetwood. The prime reason is that drivers prefer the conventional cab layout of the motor car rather than the cramped cab of the trailer. Furthermore, driving from the trailer you are divorced from the sounds of the motors and compressor and have to throw off for breakers later as the pantograph is further behind. Overall they are not popular with the crews. Their acceleration is slower than other cars due to the dead weight of the trailer and the interlocks between the doors and the controller means that the doors have to be closed before the car can move, costing vital seconds.

Around 1997 the usage pattern of the Twin Cars changed. They tended to make their debut in early June, rather than mid-July and were favoured on specials due to the higher proportion of elderly passengers visiting at that time. Many would refuse to climb the stairs of a Balloon Car. As a result they saw more use than in previous years, although this seemed to depend more on the availability of staff than anything else. For very many years the Twin Cars were stored on tracks 12 and 13 of the depot (the seventh set would use any spare track). The logic presumably was that as these were amongst the least used cars, there would be little need to remove the mobile tram wash (which would foul their exit). During 1998 they were generally stored on pits 2 and 3, although by 2000 they once again were on 12 and 13.

As noted above, most journeys are made between loops, however there are probably more trailer leading journeys now than in previous years. Particularly when cars are used on early season evening specials when there is little need for extras north of Cabin, Twin Cars can be found using most turning points. They can cross anywhere, although to turn at Cleveleys they have to completely cross the road junction, change ends and return to use the cross over. As travelling wrong line over an unsignalled road crossing is generally frowned upon, Twin Cars would normally continue to Thornton Gate.

Opposite: Although so much smarter than it had been at the end of the 1980s, 683 was starting to look a little shabby in 2001, eleven years after its last repaint. Several Twin Cars retained the 1990s posters next to their doors encouraging safe crossing of the tram tracks. (James Millington)

Left: *The 1990s livery was simple and effective - although it did seem to vary in detail over time. 671 shows off its new windscreen and yellow on black blind in this 2000 shot at Little Bispham. Once they had been permanently coupled the trams could operate almost any journey of any length yet the familar pattern of Pleasure Beach - Little Bispham still reigned supreme. It is often wondered how many times 281+T1 or 671+681, for example, have been around this loop? 5,000?*

Opposite: *677 - the only motor car to be scrapped - shows evidence of minor accident repairs to its skirt in this 2001 shot at Waterloo Road. (James Millington x 2)*

Right: *By 2001 a shabby 685 had lost its fleet number. It has just arrived at Little Bispham from Pleasure Beach ready to push 674+684 off the loop.*
(James Millington)

Opposite: *684 stood out thanks to this wonky fleet number. This was the first set to receive the new style windscreens in 1997 - (678 to 680 had already been treated by this time). (James Millington)*

Top: *673 shows the scars of battle in this 2002 view with a checker plate patch on the cab corner. 673 and 676 both had their couple boxes panelled over, giving a neater look. This 2002 scene at Broadwater shows the more rural aspect of the Blackpool Tramway. From the hustle and bustle of the Promenade, with frequent stops and short journeys, a full length run to Fleetwood was often the preferred choice for a Twin, particularly on Market days and moreso on Tuesdays. Even as recently as 1999, it was commonplace for all seven sets to run to Fleetwood two or three times on every Tuesday in July and August, conveying holidaymakers in search of bargains. By comparison, a decade on, and there were no Twin Cars at all to Fleetwood on any Tuesday in summer 2009. (James Millington)*

Bottom: *2004 was 676s last season - despite having the most recent truck overhaul - it missed out on the Metro repaints and was placed into store. It managed a few appearances in 2004 - although its re-liveried sisters tended to dominate. A loose windscreen seemed to plague its final days though. The tram passes through Manchester Square on 31st August 2004. (Brian Turner)*

TWIN CARS' FINEST HOUR

The finest hour of the Twin Cars coincided with what was arguably the lowest ebb of the Blackpool Tramway. Due to its age, the tram track on the section between Thornton Gate and Ash Street became the subject of a 16mph speed limit during 2002. On 17th October a further restriction was imposed, banning double deck cars on this section. The following day's service had been scheduled for double deck operation with two conductors on each tram. With the ban in place, the only option was to use the Twin Cars. They had seen use on timetabled service before, particularly on Starr Gate to Bispham operation in the 1970s and occasionally on Fleetwood service in the same period - but this was the first scheduled use since then. On 18th October 2002 the nine car service used all seven Twin Cars and two Brush Cars:

Route 1	673+683	Route 6	630
Route 2	632	Route 7	675+685
Route 3	672+682	Route 8	674+684
Route 4	671+681	Route 9	677+687
Route 5	676+686		

672+682 were first out, operating the 05.39 Manchester Square to Fleetwood journey and were also the last to return to depot at 01.20. With nine trips to Fleetwood and 19 hours 40 minutes use, this was probably the longest day's work of their history. Twin Cars saw occasional use on service and specials for the remainder of the season.

During winter 2002/03 trackwork was undertaken which saw around half of the restricted section renewed. This was insufficient to remove the double decker ban and it was clear that the Twin Cars would see intensive use during 2003. To prepare them it was decided to commence a repaint programme. Blackpool's buses had been route branded from April 2001 using a standard livery layout, but with different base colours. It was decided to use these liveries to brighten up the tram cars.

In order to fit this around other commitments, those cars needing the least Body Shop time were chosen. 672+682 were split at the end of January and were repainted orange and yellow in the style of Line 1 - the Promenade bus service. Work undertaken involved the replacement of 672s trolley tower, panelling out of the 'inner' end destinations, fitting of saloon heaters and re-upholstery of the seat cushions. 671+681 followed during March and received

Line 2 livery of light green and yellow - but retained its old seat cushions. Both received route branding with 'T' logos where the service number would normally appear. 672+682 made their debut on Good Friday, followed by 671+681 on the following day - and ran over Easter before the branding could be applied. It had been expected that 674+684 would be painted too, and indeed it received minor panelling attention in the Fitting Shop. However at Easter it operated with its new panels painted in primer. It finally entered the Paint Shop in May and returned to use in June, resplendent in Line 4 Cadbury blue and yellow. Extensive use of Twin Cars - up to four per day - on Fleetwood service commenced in May and frequently cars ran trailer leading - much more so than in previous seasons, when every effort (especially by drivers) had been made to get motor cars at the front.

The next repaint was 673+683 which took place during September and they emerged in Line 11 turquoise and yellow. Work then commenced on 675+685 with both cars seeing some bodywork attention towards the end of the season. However it was not until September 2004 that repaint work began and 675+685 missed the entire summer season as they were outshopped in Line 5 red and yellow just prior to its close. Earlier in 2004 Blackpool Transport introduced a new ruling which required the use of high intensity headlight-fitted cars north of Thornton Gate after dark. As the Twin Cars already featured the low voltage inverter required to power these, 674+684 had halogen headlamps and tail lamps fitted in January 2004 - tastefully done using the original mountings. Sets 1, 2 and 3 soon followed with 675+685 making five after its repaint. Double deckers were now permitted to return to Fleetwood but Twin Cars still made frequent appearances on service. Sadly just two years after their finest hour, the two unrepainted Twin Cars were withdrawn at the end of the 2004 season as part of a general fleet reduction which saw off many Brush Cars as well. After quite sporadic use all summer, both 676+686 and 677+687 last ran on 23rd October 2004.

The 2005 season again saw quite regular use of the five surviving Twin Cars on Fleetwood service, helped by several of the Balloons receiving repaints with attendant spells out of use. The season had an earlier than usual start with the appearance of 671+681, 672+682, 674+684 and later 675+685 on Fleetwood service on Maundy Thursday - rare pre-Easter use (if only by one day!). The Twin Cars' winter training use had been spiced up somewhat by the unusual use of Blundell Street and Princess Street to access the depot while the main points at Manchester Square were replaced. The diversion was in place from January until just before Easter, then again from Easter until the end of April. 671+681 and 672+682 used the route while on training duties and both, together with 673+683, 675+685, 678 and 680 used it during April to take up service. 678 also performed at a special 'By Tram to the Foxhall' event carrying passengers in aid of charity. The only known previous passenger run by a Twin Car on this route was with 675+685 on 28th June 1998 - the occasion of a depot open day as part of the Tramroad Centenary celebrations. 673+683 had tested the route two days before.

The 2006 season started quietly for the Twin Cars. Overhaul work on Balloon 713 and Jubilee 762 provided a pool of 11 high intensity headlamp fitted double deckers for the seven summer Fleetwood workings. The five twin sets were now only to be used when double deckers were unavailable. 674+684 handled most of the winter training duties and consequently became the last to enter passenger service in late July. Sets 1 and 2 seemed to do the lion's share of the passenger work, with 675+685 probably the least used. In 2007 it was announced that all five sets would be stored until July - although 675+685 did make appearances on training during the spring. After a few years of more widespread use, the Twin Cars were back to their summer peak duties. Set 5 was the designated driver trainer during the spring, sets 1 and 4 duly launched Twin Car operation for the year on 1st July with sets 2 and 3 following later in the month. A mix of specials and service duties occupied the cars.

Sadly 2007 is also remembered for the demise of the first production motor car 677. Blackpool Transport received a Heritage Lottery Fund grant to restore the Western Train, and as the locomotive was dismantled it became clear that major attention would be required to the passenger saloon - formed from a half saloon of Railcoach 209. It was decided to use the saloon of another car rather than build a new frame, and 677 was selected as a donor. It also allowed a set of traditionally sprung trucks to be released for 733, replacing the ex-OMO car Metalastik trucks used since the 1980s. During early June it was admitted to the Fitting Shop for initial stripping before the trucks were replaced by a slave set. On 20th June it moved to the Body Shop and was quickly stripped to a shell. Early July saw it reduced to just a half saloon dumped in the depot once more. 733s new underframe was ready to receive 677s saloon on 9th October and the swap was accomplished in the tram depot. 677s underframe was then shunted into the Fitting Shop where it was cut up for scrap at the grand old age of 72. Its bereaved trailer, 687, faced life as a store vehicle in the depot, stripped of its seats.

The 2008 season saw a further decline in Twin Car use. The first passenger working was 673+683 on 3rd May, but other than driver training no sets saw action until July. 673+683 and 675+685 were the most commonly used cars on training and service, although 672+682 did put in at least one training duty. 674+684 were hired for a tram tour in October, but it was not until the final week of the season that use intensified with Sets 2, 3, 4 and 5 all in use. 671+681 are believed to have operated on a test run but not in service.

Other than a rare January private hire with 673+683 (see page 74) the 2009 season kicked off with private hires. May 3rd saw Sets 2 and 5 on an enthusiasts tour, while 675+685 also appeared on a hire on 25th June with a brief period on specials afterwards. 672+682 ran on two tours in September and it was not until October 3rd that regular use began with Sets 2, 3 and 5 on specials. At least one set appeared every Saturday in October, midweek use then occurred during October half term week and Set 3 ended the season on Sunday 8th November on an enthusiast tour as part of the 'Farewell to Fleetwood' events - maybe its last visit to Fleetwood Ferry due to the temporary closure of the street sections until 2012. Sadly 674+684 joined 671+681 in store during the year and did not appear in service. Only 36 workings were recorded for the entire year, of which nine were private hires.

During 2009, work began on the major upgrade of the Blackpool Tramway and an order was placed for 16 new low floor trams. 2010 dawned with much of the tram fleet under threat - disposals of the stored cars were beginning and 687 was quickly acquired by the Lancastrian Transport Trust as a spares donor. In February they also acquired 676+686 for preservation - saving one of the two prototype sets. Sets 1 to 5 were to be retained until the end of the 2011 season as their 2003 overhauls left them with some residual book value. Only 672+682 and 675+685 were to be prepared for use during 2010 - the other three sets now faced a future in store. Remarkably expressions of interest were received for all five sets. 672+682 will join the Tramway Museum Society collection at Crich; 674+684 have been reserved by a consortium of tramway and railway enthusiasts from Cumbria and 673+683 and 675+685 by private individuals. 672+682 launched the Twin Cars' season on 7th April on a Tram Driver Experience - a new initative launched by Blackpool Transport during the 2009 season.

So 2010 is a bittersweet year - the 50th anniversary of the production Twin Sets, yet just two remain active and there seems little prospect of an upturn in their fortunes. Only one further season remains before the tramway upgrade is complete and the surviving sets head to new homes. Fortunately 676+686 are in secure local ownership and hopefully can demonstrate the UKs most successful trailer car design in the years to come.

THE METRO REPAINTS

Repainting a Twin Car is a complicated process. Normally both cars are done together to ensure they are both fresh and also because uncoupling them is a complex job. The application of Metro liveries in 2002 demonstrated this.

Above: *682 shows the level of preparation with extensive rubbing down and the first primer applied to the roof. Little panel work had been undertaken as the car was last repainted in 1998.*

Top right: *672 has been undercoated in the new style. The Twin Car glass has been removed for recolouring to match the new livery.*

Bottom right: *682 has now received its orange and yellow gloss. Note how the colour divide below the windows is higher on the trailer than the motor in an attempt to pair up the two halves. (James Millington x 3)*

Left: In 50 years of operation there have only been a handful of occasions when motors and trailers of the same set have stood side by side. Even then this was usually within the confines of the workshops, making photography difficult or actually impossible. There are no known images of any cream liveried cars alongside each other, likewise, very few exist in the half green and half cream livery. These two images must rate as some of the rarest ever recorded and although only a few years old, by comparison to others in the book, they will never be repeated again. This is 671+681 together in the Body Shop. Note how the trailer had retained its disused destination glass - this was removed from both cars of Sets 1 to 5 during their 2003/04 Metro repaints.

Right: 673+683 share the two Body Shop tracks in August 2003. This was a somewhat surprising time to split and repaint a Twin Set, just before the Illuminations in a year when double deck cars were prohibited from operating to Fleetwood! Fortunately the works pulled out all the stops and the set was back in service on 1st October in Line 11 turquoise and yellow. Note the missing hoses from 683.
(James Millington x 2)

Top: 673 was the fourth motor to receive Metro livery, gaining the attractive turquoise and yellow scheme for Line 11. As with the other repainted cars, the redundant blind glass and 'Progress Twin Car' legend had been removed and replaced with a plain panel. The unoccupied head and tail lamp apertures remained unscathed though - nearly forty years after they were last required. The rear window was transferred from the trailer when the set was permanently coupled in 1965 and here provides a useful hook to tie the cables to.

Bottom: The final Metro repaint was 675+685. These required quite extensive work, as shown here on 675 in the Body Shop. New windscreens were made and the entire cab repanelled. The work was spread out over much of 2004 so that the set missed the entire season.

Opposite: 672+682 had the honour of making the first Metro liveried Twin Car journey on Good Friday, 18th April 2003. The trams left depot with 682 leading and ran to Tower. With 672 now leading, the trams ran to Pleasure Beach before working two consecutive journeys to Little Bispham and back before it was time for the crew meal break. Seen at Little Bispham first time round, the vivid livery contrasts with the air of neglect at the turning circle. Fortunately the Metro logo was soon repositioned and this attention to detail lifted the whole appearance of the car end.
(James Millington x 3)

Left: *Resplendent in Line 5 red and yellow, 675+685 finally made it out for the 2005 season. 685 was one of three motors (with 671 and 674) to receive drip trays to catch the grease from their pantographs, located at the top of the tower. Twin Cars on New South Promenade, whilst not particularly rare, became much more common after 2002 when they appeared on Fleetwood service more regularly. (Nick Meskell)*

Below: *671+681 received Line 2 light green and yellow, and their paintwork was perhaps the most restrained of the technicolour fleet. The drip tray is helping to keep the livery smart in this May 2004 shot at Cleveleys. (James Millington)*

Opposite: *May 2008 saw an early appearance for 683+673 on specials. They are seen here storming through the fields at Rossall. This is the section which requires high intensity headlights at night, as fitted to Sets 1 to 5 in 2004. (David Umpleby)*

Below: *674+684 was the third set repainted into Metro livery, adopting the Line 4 scheme of Cadbury blue and yellow. The set returned to use in June 2003, but on 10th August 2004, 684 suffered accident damage to the rear. Repairs were quickly effected but the new panel omitted both the Metro logo and the fleet number. The blue below the windscreen was applied to a deeper level too. (Nick Meskell)*

Opposite: *682 and 685 sit side by side on Pleasure Beach loop during an enthusiasts tour in May 2009. Closer inspection shows some minor detail differences - particularly the later use of flat beading on 682 compared to the half round on 685 and the headlights. (David Umpleby)*

ON THE INSIDE

Top: Here is the cab of 675. The drivers seat is resting against the controller case - this is lowered once the driver is in the cab. The English Electric Z-type controller is in the traditional angled position with the drivers timetable (known as the route card in Blackpool-speak) propped up behind it. The air brake is centrally mounted with the black and silver handle. To its left is a rocker switch for the door and light direction controls with air pressure and air reservoir gauges below. Two red lights beside the brake handle identify when the doors are open.

Bottom: This 2008 view shows the driving cab of trailer 685. The controller is on the left, brake handle in the centre and hand brake wheel on the right. The lights on the facia denote that the doors are open. The gauge on the right shows air pressure. The plunger below it works the windscreen washers. The rocker switch to the right of the gauge sets the headlights to main or dipped beam. On the floor the large pedal controls the sanders in the motor whilst the small round ones are the air whistle and the lifeguard reset pedal. (Brian Turner x 2)

The three basic motor car interiors are shown here.

Above: *676 shows the brilliant white darvic ceiling on this car resulting from the removal of its sliding roof in 1969.*

Top Right: *The inside of 672 and most of the motors retain this style with varnished wood (cream painted on 671 and 674) window frames, wood effect formica sides (as on the cab door) and cream painted hardboard ceilings.*

Bottom Right: *675 shows the effect of the missing roof windows with hardboard panelling in place. This and 676 feature turquoise Panax laminates with cream laminates on the windows. Lime green moquette has replaced the earlier dark green on this car and the first row of seats have been fixed to accomodate saloon heaters. Change for notes is not guaranteed - an edict which became progressively less reasonable with each annual fare rise. (James Millington x 3)*

Above: The number 2 end of 672 shows the bench seat created where the former driving controls were. Underneath the seats remains various switch equipment which can be heard whilst the car is operating. The grille in the centre is for the saloon heaters fitted in 2003. This car had a full retrim in the later lime green moquette. Note the disused destination box. (Nick Meskell)

Left: 682 shows the driving end of a trailer with the full height cab door and part height bulkheads. Note the alhambrinal ceiling panels and the flat-topped seat cushions compared to the curved-topped style of the motors. (Brian Turner)

Top Left: The conductor's door controls on 672 include the original push buttons alongside the bell push. The red light above identifies that either the motor or trailer doors or both are open.

Bottom Left: By contrast 682 has been retro-fitted with plainer buttons and hand written identification.

Top Right: A well known feature of Blackpool's trams are the strident instructions traditionally carried. Woe betide the poor passenger who dares to open the doors. The red light again signifies an open door.

Bottom Right: The emergency brake and air gauge on 682s bulkhead. (David Umpleby x 4)

A NARROW ESCAPE FOR 681

Top: *On Tuesday 15th July 1997, 671+681 were unloading at St Chad's Road on a southbound journey to Pleasure Beach when 644 failed to stop and ran into them. (See page 52). The resulting deformation is clear and the tram was dragged back to depot. 644 skulks at the rear of the neighbouring track.*

Bottom: *It was not until April 1998 that 681 was admitted to the works for repairs which lasted until October 1998. After reconnection in March, the set finally returned to service on 11th June 1999 - 23 months after the accident. This 2001 shot shows the smaller corner side windows and the slightly misshapen dome. (James Millington)*

THE DEMISE OF 677

On Wednesday 27th October 2004, 677+687 returned to depot for the final time. Along with several other redundant trams they began to gather dust. 677 was rudely awakened from its slumbers in June 2007 when it was moved into the Fitting Shop to be stripped down as it had been selected to provide body parts for the restoration of the Illuminated Western train.

Right: 677 was shunted from the Fitting Shop to the Body Shop on 20th June 2007 on accommodation trucks and shorn of much of its equipment. (David Umpleby)

Below: A few weeks later and this was all that remained. The surviving saloon was soon to be transferred onto 733s new underframe and the remains of 677 were then scrapped. (David Umpleby)

Below Right: 687 became a store in the depot. (Nick Meskell)

TWINS AROUND FOXHALL

The track on Princess Street from Foxhall Square to Blundell Street is the only surviving section of the original 1885 conduit route and as the main access route to Blundell Street depot, it saw daily use until Rigby Road depot took over in 1935. Infrequent use continued, especially in the summer, until the 1960s when a new entrance was opened onto Rigby Road. Since then Princess Street and Blundell Street have seen little use. Enthusiast specials were quite frequent in the 1970s and 1980s, but other than an event in 1998 the line has been virtually dormant since.

Track renewal at Manchester Square junction in 2005 changed all this. On 11th January trams left for service along Blundell Street and Princess Street and continued to do so every day until 23rd March and then again after Easter from 4th to 29th April. 672+682 operated regularly on driver training from January and 671+681, 673+683, 675+685 also used the route to enter service during April.

Above: The second phase of operation saw Twin Cars in use on Fleetwood service. On 22nd April, 673 swings slowly round the corner from Blundell Street into Princess Street behind Centenary 647. (Nick Meskell)

Left: 672+682 saw regular use for Twin Car familiarisation as part of the tram driving school. Other than special runs for the 1998 event, this was believed to be the first time a Twin Set has used the route. 682 leads its sister across a blustery Promenade on 19th January 2005. (Brian Turner)

Opposite: On 16th April, 671+681 return to depot under the watchful eye of two passers-by and the overhead line crew on 754 behind. (Brian Turner)

ON A WET WINTER'S NIGHT

Winter appearances of Twin Cars are normally confined to driver training with the odd enthusiast hire. On 27th January 2009 a private party of over 100 people were taken from the Imperial Hotel to North Pier. This was too many for a Balloon so 673+683 were used. Their return journey left at 00.15 the following morning. With a foreshortened tram service (Pleasure Beach to Little Bispham) the last service car arrived in depot at 23.42 and just after midnight Set 3 left depot with the tramway to itself.

Right: 673s lights pierce the gloom over a deserted Lytham Road as the car waits to cross the Promenade road and head for North Pier to collect its party.

Below: The short journey is over and the party has dashed to the Imperial Hotel. Only the photographer braves the elements as 683 waits to leave for Cabin where it would reverse and lead its partner home. (Paul Turner x 2)

TWINS AT NIGHT

Left: *The roof windows of the Twin Cars are shown to best effect after dark. On 1st November 2008, 674+684 wait at Cleveleys on a Fleetwood to Manchester Square working. The bright halogen headlights will point the way back to depot on what turned out to be 674+684s last ever passenger journey in Blackpool, as it did not reappear for the 2009 season. (Jason Cross)*

Right: *On the same day 675+685 operated on specials. The previous winter had seen the loops remodelled at the Pleasure Beach with the trams on the inner and outer loops now facing in the same direction. What had in recent years become a desolate place has been transformed as part of the town's sea defence work. (Jason Cross)*

No.	1968 No.	New	Into Service	Coupled	Pantograph	Half Green/Cream Repaints	1990s Green/Cream Repaints	Metro Livery	Withdrawn	Notes
281	671	Nov 1960	Dec 1960	Oct 1962	Feb 1990	Nov 1964	Feb 90/Jul 98	Mar 2003	Sep 2007	Stored
T 1	681	Jul 1960	Jul 1960	Oct 1962	-	Nov 1964	Jan 90/Nov 98	Mar 2003	Sep 2007	Stored
272	672	Sep 1960	Sep 1960	Dec 1964	Apr 1991	Dec 1964	May 91/Jul 98	Feb 2003	-	
T 2	682	Aug 1960	Aug 1960	Dec 1964	-	Dec 1964	Apr 91/Jun 98	Feb 2003	-	
273	673	May 1961	Jul 1961	Jan 1965	May 1990	Jan 1965	May 1990	Sep 2003	Nov 2009	Stored
T 3	683	Sep 1960	Sep 1960	Jan 1965	-	Jan 1965	Jun 1990	Sep 2003	Nov 2009	Stored
274	674	May 1962	May 1962	Jan 1965	Oct 1991	Feb 1965/Oct 1973	Nov 91/Aug 97	May 2003	Nov 2008	Stored
T 4	684	Oct 1960	Oct 1960	Jan 1965	-	Jan 1965/Oct 1973	Nov 91/Aug 97	May 2003	Nov 2008	Stored
275	675	Mar 1958	Apr 1958	May 1965	Jun 1990	Apr 1965/Sep 1980	Jul 1990	Sep 2004	-	275 a trailer 1958-Mar 1961
T 5	685	Oct 1960	Apr 1961	May 1965	-	May 1965	Jul 1990	Oct 2004	-	
276	676	Mar 1958	Apr 1958	Nov 1969	Oct 1991	Aug 1969	Aug 1991	-	Oct 2004	Stored
T 6	686	Nov 1960	Apr 1961	Nov 1969	-	Nov 1969	Oct 1991	-	Oct 2004	Stored
277	677	Jun 1960	Jul 1960	Jul 1970	Jun 1991	Jul 1970	Jan 1992	-	Oct 2004	Scrapped Jul 2007
T 7	687	Nov 1960	Apr 1961	Jul 1970	-	Jul 1970	Jan 1992	-	Oct 2004	Stored
278	678	Jul 1961	Aug 1961	-	Oct 1988	Mar 71/Oct 73/Dec 78	Mar 1993	-	Oct 2006	Stored. Panto Jul 75-Jul 76
T 8	688	Dec 1960	Jun 1962	-	-	Jan 1972	-	-	Sep 1972	Scrapped Oct 1992
279	679	Apr 1961	May 1961	-	Aug 1985	Jan 1971/Oct 1973	Jun 1999	-	Nov 2004	To LTT Apr 2009
T 9	689	Jan 1961	May 1961	-	-	Dec 1971	-	-	Sep 1972	To GEC Traction Jan 1981
280	680	Dec 1960	Feb 1961	-	Dec 1988	Dec 1970/Oct 1973	Mar 1992	-	Oct 2008	Stored for Heaton Park
T10	690	Jan 1961	Apr 1961	-	-	Dec 1971	-	-	Sep 1972	To GEC Traction Jan 1981

Other repaints:

678: 1980s Green/Cream - Jun 1984; Camelot - Apr 1988; North West Auto Trader - May 1990; Pleasure Beach Paradise Room - Apr 1995; Royal British Legion - Aug 1997 and Feb 2000; Radio Wave - Jul 2004.

679: 1980s Green/Cream - Jul 1985; Isle of Man Funboat - Mar 1987 and Jun 1991; Mecca Bingo - Jul 1994; Seagull Coaches - Jul 1995; 1980s Green/Cream - Feb 2004.

680: 1980s Green/Cream - Jun 1985; Scruffy Murphy's - Aug 1995; Dillons Bookstore - Jul 1996; Leonard Cheshire - Mar 1998; Central Pier - Jul 2004; Merrie England Bar - Jul 2006; Base blue - Mar 2008.

Left: *As the 2009 season drew to a close the three operational Twin sets saw occasional use during the Illuminations period. On 22nd October 2009 682+672 have arrived at Bispham from Pleasure Beach as dusk approaches. (Jason Cross)*

Overleaf: *The sun sets on the Twin Cars - just two sets remain in use for 2010, and after 2011 there will be none. 672+682 bask on Little Bispham loop. (Jason Cross).*

Back cover: *A magical Twin Car moment at North Pier from 2006 with 685+675 loading for Fleetwood while 671+681, chased by Engineering Car 754 head south. (Nick Meskell)*

All rights reserved. No part of this book may be reproduced or transmitted in any form or by any means, electronic or mechanical, including photocopying, scanning, recording or by any information storage and retrieval system, without written permission from the publisher.
Published by Train Crazy c/o Videoscene, PO Box 243, Lytham St. Annes. FY8 9DE. Telephone: 01253 738336. Email: sales@videoscene.co.uk
Visit www.tramsmagazine.co.uk for more details of our Blackpool tram products or call in at The Blackpool Tram Shop at North Pier, Blackpool.